World Cup 2022, Built on 6500 Skulls and Hate?

How Qatar Bribed the Football World, Uses Modern Slavery, and Promotes Inequality

Edition 3.0

REBEL PRESS MEDIA

Disclaimer

FIFA denies accusations

Gianni Infantino remarkably denies that at least 6,500 people were killed in the construction of the World Cup stadiums in Qatar, as previously reported to the Guardian by various authorities. According to the FIFA president, the actual death toll is only three. "And that is still three too many," Infantino said at the Council of Europe in Strasbourg, which had invited the FIFA president.

The Guardian calculated in February 2021 that at least 6,500 people were killed in Qatar during work for the upcoming World Cup. These were migrant workers who, for example, were building the stadiums, or airports that were supposed to be there for the tournament. The total number of deaths was reported by India, Pakistan, Nepal, Bangladesh and Sri Lanka; the five Asian countries where many migrant workers come from. It is likely that the total number of deaths is much higher because many workers also come from the Philippines and Kenya, for example. Those countries have not disclosed figures.

So these are death rates reported by the countries from which the migrant workers come. Infantino, however, seems to blame "the media. "I have to correct some things," the Swiss said in Strasbourg. "I can still accept it from some of the media, but I also hear here today that 6,500 people died in Qatar. That is simply not true. The real figures are: three people died. And that's still three too many." Infantino does not provide any substantiation for that claim.

Infantino also disputes that workers in Qatar have to work in deplorable conditions, as has been extensively reported in various international media. "With work, we give people dignity," the FIFA boss said. "The working conditions are the same as in Europe." Infantino also caused a stir a day earlier with statements about African refugees.

At the Strasbourg meeting, Infantino defended his plan to hold a biennial World Cup. In doing so, the FIFA boss insinuated that his idea could ensure that fewer African migrants die while crossing into Europe. Infantino said that "soccer can help improve people's lives all over the world. "We need to give people hope with this kind of project so that they don't want to flee anymore," he said. Infantino rectified those quotes moments later, saying he was speaking generally about plans that can contribute to the development of the continent of Africa.

Table of Contents

Disclaimer	1
FIFA denies accusations	2
Table of Contents	4
The history of FIFA accusations	5
A past of scandals?	8
World cup ambassador is homophobic?	12
Arrests in Qatar	14
Qatar forces migrant workers to move?	16
Amnesty international is pissed off!	19
Ultimatum for FIFA	21
History repeats itself?	24
The scandals of south Africa and Brazil?	28
The morality of hypocrisy?	34
How did it happen in Qatar?	36
Slaves or workers?	44
FIFA must take responsibility?	49
Qatar wants to buy recognition?	56
The rules in Qatar	58

The history of FIFA accusations

Fourteen people, nine of whom are connected to the governing body of global soccer, FIFA, were indicted in May 2015 by the U.S. Federal Bureau of Investigation (FBI) on suspicion of bribery, extortion and money laundering over a period of several years. Seven FIFA officials were arrested May 27 at the Hotel Baur au Lac, Zurich. They are expected to be extradited to the United States on suspicion of receiving $150,000,000 in bribes.

The arrests took place around the 65th FIFA Congress at which a new president for the soccer organization was to be elected. Several soccer associations, particularly those in Europe, demanded the departure of sitting president Sepp Blatter. However, Blatter did not withdraw, defeating his opposing candidate Prince Ali in the presidential election with 133 out of 209 votes. A few days later, he still announced his departure, saying he did not have the support of the entire soccer world.

The arrests mainly revolve around suspicions of bribery, fraud and money laundering in the allocation of media and marketing rights for FIFA matches in the Americas and at the 2016 Copa América Centenario in the United States. Allegations also refer to bribery in sponsorship of soccer apparel, in the selection process for the host country for the 2010 World Cup and in the 2011 FIFA presidential election.

Chuck Blazer, a former CONCACAF official, helped the FBI with the investigation after his secret guilty plea in a 2013 trial.

On Dec. 21, FIFA's ethics committee suspended Sepp Blatter and Michel Platini for eight years for violating the code of ethics. Blatter will also be fined 50,000 Swiss francs and Platini must pay 80,000 Swiss francs. Both are barred from all soccer-related activities at the national and international level.

In May 2016, it was revealed that Sepp Blatter and two other former FIFA executives enriched themselves with 72 million euros. They are Jerome Valcke, FIFA's former secretary general, and Markus Kattner, who was financial director of the world football federation. The three former top FIFA executives allegedly gave themselves and each other hefty annual salary increases, allocated World Cup bonuses and divided other bonuses among themselves. According to FIFA, there was a coordinated modus operandi among the trio, who were previously forced to resign due to the bribery and corruption scandal at the world soccer federation. All these financial surcharges did not match the figures in the official records.

FIFA handed over the results of the internal investigation to the public prosecutor's office in Switzerland. The world soccer federation will also inform the U.S. Justice Department. Both agencies are investigating malpractice at FIFA.

In mid-2019, Jack Warner, former vice president of FIFA, was sentenced by a New York judge to a hefty fine of US$79 million. The case had been brought by CONCACAF, the soccer federation of North and Central America and the Caribbean where Warner was in charge until his suspension in 2011. Warner was accused of embezzlement and corruption and was suspended for life by the world soccer federation. Warner is still out on bail in Trinidad and Tobago, but the United States has an extradition request pending against him.

A past of scandals?

The arrest of six FIFA officials marked a huge scandal for the world soccer federation. In recent years, the association has rolled from one incident to another.

The ISL scandal: Between 1992 and 2000, the company ISL paid bribes to FIFA officials, including then Brazilian president Joao Havelange. The marketing company bought broadcast rights to important events for millions and resold them. Top FIFA officials pocketed "substantial sums of money," a 2013 investigation revealed. Current president Sepp Blatter got off scot-free, even though investigators wondered aloud whether he must not have known about the corruption.

Election 1998: The presidential election shortly before the World Cup in France is not without suspicions. Blatter defeats Swede Lennart Johansson and becomes president. Prior to the election, it is rumored that African delegates were bribed at a hotel in Paris. Blatter has always dismissed that accusation.

The 2018 and 2022 World Cups: Bribes were allegedly paid to FIFA from Russia and Qatar, the organizers of the 2018 and 2022 World Cups, to secure those tournaments. In 2010, both countries were actually awarded the organization. FIFA later investigated the many bribery allegations, but concluded last year that there were no gross violations of the rules. This outcome is also being questioned.

Election 2011: Blatter found a serious challenger in the FIFA presidency in 2011 in the person of Mohammed bin Hammam of Qatar. Bin Hammam withdrew from the election, however, because he was accused of bribery. He allegedly bribed Caribbean officials in his hunt for the presidency. At the same time, there are allegations that Bin Hammam transferred money to officials for the organization of the World Cup in Qatar. Qatar's federation denies that.

World Cup tickets: Several times FIFA officials went into the black market with World Cup tickets, according to allegations. The main suspect is Jack Warner from Trinidad and Tobago, who has been named in numerous FIFA scandals. He allegedly resold tickets in 2002 and 2006 and made big money from them. Ismail Bhamjee of Botswana also allegedly resold tickets in 2006. In 2014, the son of Argentine FIFA top official Julio Grondona allegedly resold tickets.

1973 - João Havelange in power
João Havelange wielded the scepter as FIFA president from 1973 to 1998. The now 99-year-old Brazilian, more or less Blatter's mentor, reportedly did not come to power in a very clean way.

German investigative journalist Thomas Kistner writes in his book FIFA Mafia that Havelange bribed African board members to remove Briton Stanley Rous from the throne as FIFA's top boss. Horst Dassler, the son of the founder of Adidas, allegedly had a hand in this. Dassler is known as the founder of commerce in sports. The "close cooperation" between FIFA and marketing company ISL can also be credited to Havelange and Dassler.

FIFA expert Andrew Jennings also already accused Havelange of corruption. The Brazilian allegedly took gigantic bribes for marketing and TV contracts.

1986 - ISL bribes senior FIFA officials for broadcast rights
Indeed, Dassler founded marketing company ISL himself. The Swiss organization paid tens of millions of euros in bribes to senior FIFA officials to buy the broadcasting rights to World Cups, for example.

As a result, former president Havelange was allowed to credit over a million euros in bribes to his bank account. This all came out in a court case, after which Havelange handed in his honorary presidency of FIFA in 2013. Blatter was still secretary general at the time and denied any involvement.

By the way, ISL no longer exists. The company went bankrupt in 2001 due to skyrocketing debts.

1992 - Morocco attempts bribery for 1998 World Cup. France was awarded the 1998 World Cup, but rival Morocco allegedly made attempts to bribe. This is according to a statement by former board member

Chuck Blazer to the FBI. It is not known whether France also laid down money to secure the tournament.

1998 - 'Blatter elected with bribes'
In 1998, Blatter succeeded his mentor Havelange as FIFA president. He defeated Swedish UEFA president Lennart Johansson, but that election battle was not entirely smooth. Bribes were reportedly handed out to African executives so they would vote for Blatter.

One African even allegedly left his envelope of money at the hotel by mistake. Blatter waved away all accusations.

World cup ambassador is homophobic?

Qatari former soccer player Khalid Salman, ambassador for the World Cup that begins Nov. 20 in his country, has made unkind remarks about the LGBTQ+ community and women in a German documentary. He called homosexuality "mental harm."
Furthermore, LGBTQ+ may come to the World Cup in his country, but must "accept Qatari rules," Salman warned. Women are better off staying home, according to him.

Qatar's World Cup ambassador made the statements in a German ZDF documentary.

That documentary will be broadcast Tuesday night.

"During the World Cup, many people enter the country. For example, gays," Salman said. "The most important thing is that everyone will accept them coming here. But they will have to accept our rules."

Salman has a particular problem with children seeing gay people because they would learn something that he believes is not right. In his view, homosexuality is haram and therefore forbidden. "It is a mental illness," he said.

The interview was quickly ended after that statement by the spokesman for the organizing committee.

Interest groups LGBTQ+ community want travel warning

The German government must issue a travel warning, the LSVD said Tuesday. The LSVD is the largest interest group for the LGBTQ+ community in Germany and comparable to the Dutch COC.

LSVD board member Alfonso Pantisano called Salman's statements "disturbing, but no surprise." "They continue to reveal the homophobic attitude of the regime in Qatar. We expect the German Foreign Ministry to issue a clear travel warning for all persons belonging to the LGBTQ+ community."

COC Netherlands also reacted to the ruling. "This is of course terrible." The organization stresses that much more is needed than the travel warning already issued by the Netherlands. "Our government, other countries, FIFA, the KNVB and everyone else involved must urgently call on Qatar to improve the human rights of LGBTQ+ persons."

The COC is not only concerned with LGBTQ+ people being able to safely travel to Qatar, but also the situation of the LGBTQ+ community in the country itself. "The same goes for addressing the human rights of women, migrant workers and others in the Gulf state."

Arrests in Qatar

Authorities of Qatar's Preventive Security Service arbitrarily arrested lesbian, gay, bisexual and transgender people, Human Rights Watch concluded Monday in an investigation. The victims were mistreated and sexually abused in prison.

Human Rights Watch (HRW) documented six cases of aggravated assault and five cases of sexual assault toward LGBTQ's in police custody between 2019 and 2022.

The victims were allegedly arrested in public places and their phones were searched. Homosexuality is illegal in Qatar.

HRW interviewed six victims, some of whom say they were abused as recently as September 2022.

Rasha Younes was involved in the interviews as an LGBTQ rights researcher at Human Rights Watch. "As Qatar prepares to host the World Cup, security forces are detaining and mistreating LGBTQ's for who they are," she said. "They apparently do so in the confidence that the abuses of the security forces will remain unreported and unchecked."

The release of transgender women required them to undergo conversion therapy at a government-sponsored "behavioral health" center.

Victims were denied legal aid
All those interviewed said they were held in an underground prison in capital Doha. Here the prisoners were mentally, verbally and physically abused. The victims were denied access to legal aid, family and medical care. All six victims interviewed said police forced them to promise to "stop immoral activities."

One of the victims was held in an isolation cell for two months without access to legal assistance. None of the six arrests were recorded, leaving relatives unaware of what had happened to the victims.

There has long been criticism of the controversial World Cup hosted in Qatar, as the country has been under fire for human rights abuses for years. According to The Guardian, thousands of workers have been killed in the construction of the stadiums. A week ago, Qatar was designated the host of the 2023 Asia Cup.

Qatar forces migrant workers to move?

Qatar has evacuated apartment buildings in the capital Doha ahead of the World Cup. The thousands of foreign workers living there are being forced to leave their apartments unannounced. Some now have to sleep on mattresses in the streets. The Gulf state wants to house soccer fans in the buildings.
According to Reuters news agency, more than a dozen large apartment buildings are involved.

The authorities had not announced the eviction in advance. The residents of one building in the Al Mansoura neighborhood, which residents said was home to 1,200 people, were told around 8 p.m. (local time) on Wednesday that they had to leave within two hours.

Around 10:30 p.m., they were literally chased out of their homes and the doors of the building were closed. Some of the men, who were not yet aware of the action, had not even returned in time to collect their belongings. "We have nowhere to go," one man told Reuters the next day.

Migrant workers must make way for soccer fans
Migrant workers who had been earning a living in the Gulf state for some time also fell victim. Mohammed, a driver from Bangladesh, said he had lived in the same neighborhood for 14 years when the municipality told

him Wednesday that he had 48 hours to leave the premises. He shared that with 38 other people.

He said workers who built the infrastructure for Qatar are being pushed aside as the tournament gets closer. "Who made the stadiums? Who made the roads? Who made everything? Bengalis, Pakistanis. Now they are making us all leave."

Host Qatar controversial for several reasons
The tournament, which begins Nov. 20, is highly controversial because of the conditions in which the mostly Asian and African workers had to work while building the necessary stadiums and infrastructure. Those conditions are said to have been so bad that many people have been injured or killed.

Not only is the construction of the stadiums controversial. There is also much criticism of human rights in the country. For example, homosexuality is banned, LGBTQ's seem to be arrested without pardon and in many hotels you can only rent a room with a partner if you are married. Qatar also allegedly bribed FIFA personnel to be allowed to host the World Cup.

A spokesman for Qatar's government stated Saturday that the evictions had nothing to do with the World Cup. The government's approach is said to be part of ongoing long-term plans to revamp parts of Doha. According to the spokesman, everyone has since been given new accommodation and requests to leave "have been carried out with proper notice."

Amnesty international is pissed off!

Amnesty International on Friday reacted furiously to FIFA's remarkable letter signed by President Gianni Infantino. In the letter, the world soccer federation called on all World Cup nations to "focus entirely on soccer."

"If Infantino wants the world to 'focus on soccer,' there is a simple solution: FIFA could start addressing the serious human rights violations for once instead of shoving them under the rug," the human rights organization wrote in a statement.

The statement is in response to FIFA's letter. In the letter, the world soccer federation asks participating World Cup countries not to engage in "ideological and political battles that exist in the world."

In the run-up to the start of the tournament, an increasing number of countries expressed criticism of Qatar in recent weeks. The emirate is mainly criticized for its poor treatment of guest workers and violation of human rights. For example, homosexuality is punishable in the emirate.

"A first step would be for FIFA to publicly advocate the establishment of a compensation fund for migrant workers and ensure that lhbtis are not discriminated against or harassed," Amnesty continued in the message.

19

Amnesty thinks FIFA should take action instead
According to Amnesty, FIFA should, on the contrary,
take action. According to the human rights organization,
the association should commit to the compensation
fund, which Qatar recently waived. The emirate's
minister previously dismissed calls for such a fund as "a
publicity stunt" by other countries.

"Hundreds of thousands of workers have been used to
make this tournament possible and their rights cannot
be forgotten or waved away. It is mind-boggling. They
deserve justice and compensation, not empty promises,
and the clock is ticking," the statement reads.

"We want these issues to be addressed before the
World Cup begins," reports the organization, which is
working with other European countries on this issue.
"We want a convincing answer, which FIFA has already
promised us several times."

Ultimatum for FIFA

The European working group in talks with FIFA on human rights has given the world soccer federation an ultimatum and wants the federation to make a statement by the end of October on a compensation fund for migrant workers who suffered during the construction of stadiums for the World Cup in Qatar.

FIFA previously promised to come clean before the summer, but with the World Cup approaching, the association remains on the sidelines on the issue.

Last Wednesday, the working group and the world soccer federation sat around the table. But that has not yet had the desired effect and so there is now a demand to come up with a statement soon.

What the consequences will be if FIFA delays again, Gijs de Jong, secretary general of the KNVB, is not yet saying. He sits on that European working group on human rights, which includes the German, English and Scandinavian soccer associations.

"We are at least going in that direction, but we will consider what we do if this is not settled," said De Jong. Who believes that FIFA will "not like the ultimatum very much," but still maintains confidence that clarity will come soon. "We have been working on it for a year and a half now. We are now five weeks before the World Cup. It's time for clarity now."

21

Last month, the KNVB, through a UEFA working group, stepped up pressure on FIFA to achieve a compensation fund for migrants. Since May, Amnesty International, Human Rights Watch and unions have been calling on FIFA to compensate workers through a fund for damages suffered. They are asking for $440 million. A number of major World Cup sponsors have also joined in.

FIFA still talks about three deaths
FIFA responded in a letter sent to the UEFA working group on Sept. 28, which is in the hands of NIS. In the letter, FIFA wrote that 't recognizes the importance of compensation for migrant workers in Qatar, and that the next of kin have been compensated for the three workers killed in the construction of the World Cup stadiums.

It has been estimated by investigative journalists and human rights organizations that thousands have been killed in construction work since the World Cup was awarded to Qatar. Ruud Bosgraaf of Amnesty International responded earlier this week to FIFA's statement that three victims would be involved. "It is about many tens of thousands of workers who died, were injured or never got their salaries paid in full."

In addition to a compensation fund, the KNVB also wants so-called migrant centers to be established in Qatar. Those centers should focus on the rights of migrant workers, even after the World Cup. Talks on this too are ongoing. "But we want commitments," says De Jong. That those are not there yet when the World Cup starts in five weeks is not surprising says De Jong, "but we want FIFA to speak out clearly.

History repeats itself?

Harassment and working in extreme weather: exploitation in construction of Russian World Cup stadiums

Workers working in Russia to build the stadiums that will host the World Cup exactly one year from now are being exploited and intimidated.

In a report released today, Human Rights Watch describes how workers from poor parts of Russia or countries like Tajikistan, Uzbekistan and Kyrgyzstan, for example, are regularly denied official contracts and sometimes not paid for months at a time. Moreover, workers work for hours without appropriate clothing in extreme conditions, with temperatures up to 25 degrees below zero.

When these working conditions are complained about, workers are threatened or sent home. And when observers from world soccer federation Fifa inspect the construction site, workers are forced to stay in their homes. The human rights organization conducted research in six of the 12 playing cities. HRW spoke with 42 workers in Moscow, St. Petersburg, Kaliningrad, Rostov, Yekaterinburg and Sochi.

Harassment, dismissal, detention
The report echoes findings of human rights organizations from just before the 2014 Sochi Olympics.

Then, too, workers were intimidated, fired when they asked for clarification and held in forced detention.

HRW denounced the Fifa's stance. So the soccer federation knew what could happen, says HRW director Minky Worden. "They knew how things are done in Russia and have an obligation to pay attention to this. That was not done."

She describes St. Petersburg, where the opening game of the Confederations Cup, the traditional preparation tournament a year before the World Cup, will be played Saturday. Research by the Norwegian magazine Josimar found that North Koreans, among others, were used "as slaves" in construction. North Koreans were also used in construction work at the Mokouse Luzhniki stadium in Moscow, a report by German television channel ARD showed last month.

Russian authorities strongly deny the allegations of human rights violations. Human rights "are used as a weapon in a political struggle," Foreign Ministry spokeswoman Maria Zakharova said recently.

'Improved system'
Fifa has had what it says has been an improved system for monitoring human rights violations for a year. A progress report came out Thursday. In 2016 and 2017, 59 visits were made to stadiums in Russia. A two-day visit is made to each stadium every quarter, Fifa said.

The league writes nothing about the results of those visits, except for the situation in St. Petersburg. Fifa recently could not deny that North Korean workers were indeed working in deplorable conditions. At an inspection in March, they were no longer present, the union said in a statement.

According to the labor union BWI, which works with the Fifa, at least 17 people have been killed in stadium construction from last year until now. That is fewer than in Qatar, which will host the World Cup in 2022 and has been widely criticized for the plight of workers, but more than previous World Cups.

As many as 17 workers die during construction of World Cup stadiums in Russia
Russia is disastrous when it comes to hosting a major sporting event. During the construction of World Cup stadiums, following the whopping 70 deaths in Sotchi, 17 workers died this time.

That comes from a Human Rights Watch report distributed Wednesday. With a year to go before the start of the World Cup, the sights are already set on human rights in Russia. For example, Human Rights Watch comes out with a scathing report on the construction of six World Cup stadiums, with workers working on them having to wait months for their wages or even sometimes not being paid at all.

Some workers even had to continue working in temperatures as low as -25 degrees Celsius without much protection. "This should be a wake-up call," Ambet Yuson, big boss of a construction workers' organization, told the New York Times.

"They already have the experience of Sotchi and they need to learn from that. If you look back at Sotchi, you can see that most of the accidents happened at the end of construction. They should know better by now."

FIFA mafia

"The FIFA promise to make human rights important is being put to the test in Russia. And FIFA is not living up to the promise," said Jane Buchanan, Human Rights Watch's director in Europe and Central Asia.

The world soccer organization said the allegations are not true. FIFA says it makes "more efforts than any other sports organization" to protect human and workers' rights.

The scandals of south Africa and Brazil?

South African journalist Craig Tanner paints a disconcerting picture of the consequences of the World Cup in South Africa and Brazil.

According to FIFA, it's one big party for everyone. But with recent bribery scandals and arrests of FIFA officials, a grim world of conflicts of interest and self-enrichment is emerging. Behind successive FIFA corruption scandals are many more problems. FIFA turns top-turnovers and profits during the World Cups.

While the organizing countries are forced to invest a lot of money in facilities for soccer fans. In return, FIFA promises the countries an upswing in tourism and local economies. But according to the population, they are paying far too high a price for the festival of soccer.

' It is a bloodthirsty club that comes in for a while, makes big promises and then leaves to go suck blood elsewhere, ' says sociology professor A. Desai of the South African University of Johannesburg about FIFA.

Romàrio de Souza Faria, the Brazilian top scorer and former soccer international who played for PSV, among others, also does not have a good word to say about the World Football Federation:

' The World Cup is for the foreigners, for the thieves who rob our country. '

More than 1,000 construction workers died
While the FBI and Swiss prosecutors investigate bribery
and World Cup allocation, preparations are underway
for the next World Cups in Russia in 2018 and Qatar in
2022. Qatar denies, but according to the international
coalition of labor unions, more than a thousand
construction workers have already died due to unsafe
work situations.

Preparations for the previous World Cups in Brazil in
2014 and South Africa in 2010 are also producing drastic
consequences.

High costs
Romàrio is now a parliamentarian in Brazil. When he
hears that Brazil may host the World Cup in 2014, he is
excited. But that doesn't last long: ' I began to follow
closely what was happening and it struck me that we
were spending twice as much as we thought on building
the soccer stadiums.' The rising costs are a thorn in the
side of many Brazilians.

For years, the government has not put a dime into
important public services such as education, housing,
and health care. Homes are also being demolished to
build infrastructure for soccer tourists.

Millions of people are taking to the streets and violent
riots with the police and military are developing. Visiting
professor C. Gaffney of the University of Rio de Janeiro:

' So in 2014, a World Cup came at the expense of a generation of schoolchildren who don't find a doctor in the emergency room.'

'Brazilian subsidizes FIFA's profits'
According to the Brazilian government, the cost was indeed money well spent and provides improvements to infrastructure. Opponents feel that the new facilities, such as airports, primarily serve the high strata of the population.

It also provides economic benefits, according to Deputy Mayor N. Campeão of São Paulo: ' All that enters Brazil through tourism, for example, are revenues for our country.' But according to visiting professor C. Gaffney of the University of Rio de Janeiro, it only costs Brazil money, while it brings FIFA a historic turnover of over 4 billion euros: ' The World Cup cost 7 billion euros of which 2 billion euros for the stadiums. So in a country with low labor costs, they build extremely expensive stadiums, but there is no money for essential infrastructure. It's basically a Brazilian subsidy for FIFA's profits.'

Useless stadiums
The 12 state-of-the-art stadiums are just coming to completion in time. The pace of work is murderous and construction and renovation leads to multiple fatalities. There are warnings in advance that at least 4 stadiums will be useless after the World Cup. For a quarter of a billion euros, for example, a stadium appears in the

middle of the remote Amazon in a city without a top club. The soccer palace is hardly used. There are plans to turn it into a prison.

Street children and vagrants brutally removed
In South Africa, too, the impressive structures for the 2010 soccer festival are now mostly empty. The Dutch team reached second place there. The euphoria is great. But even in South Africa, the story behind the scenes is less rosy. According to Amnesty International, out of sight of tourists and the media, street children and vagrants are being brutally removed from the streets.

Political commentator D. McKinley: ' I think this World Cup, as always, is all about appearances and images. Where the stadiums and what the world sees on TV are more important than what really happens behind the scenes.'

3 billion euros in revenue
Until then, the World Cup in South Africa is the most profitable soccer tournament ever. TV rights and contributions from sponsors provide FIFA with over 3 billion euros in revenue.

But for South Africa, the costs are getting out of hand, according to economist S. du Plessis: ' The original estimate was that the tournament's infrastructure would cost less than 200 million euros, but the actual cost will be closer to 2 to 3 billion euros.'

A major construction and renovation program is needed to rig up 10 stadiums that meet FIFA requirements. The South African government is paying 1 billion euros. There will be 5 new soccer arenas. Also in cities where there are already large stadiums. Now, more than five years later, maintenance costs for some unused stadiums are still running at 300,000 euros per month.

'Extreme capitalism'

The Football Association mirrored a bright future for South Africa with its high attendance, additional jobs and infrastructure improvements. But according to University of Johannesburg sociology professor A. Desai, the World Cup is a form of extreme capitalism: ' The treasury has been plundered for one historic moment. The slums remain and the jobs do not. It's throwing money down the drain.'

Furious Brazilians attack FIFA vehicles

During protests in the Brazilian city of Salvador, protesters attacked and damaged FIFA vehicles. FIFA employees in that city would also stop wearing recognizable FIFA clothing to prevent new incidents.

On Wednesday, the Uruguay-Nigeria match was in the city as part of the Confederations Cup. The continuation of the tournament in Brazil is in serious danger due to ongoing protests across the country. Various media in the South American nation are speculating about halting the event that serves as a dress rehearsal for the 2014 World Cup in the same host country.

Expensive stadiums

About 1 million Brazilians took to the streets across the country in protest against the government's financial and social mismanagement, among other things. The protesters are especially angry that extremely expensive stadiums have been built, while in their eyes nothing is being done about poverty in the country. The mass demonstrations have now entered their second week and seem to be increasing.

According to some reports, FIFA has already made an urgent appeal to the participating countries to finish the tournament as planned. For one team, players are said to have already pressured team management to go home because of growing doubts about safety, including with regard to family members living in Brazil.

The morality of hypocrisy?

Russia may not be allowed to participate in the barrages for the World Cup in Qatar at the end of March. Russia was scheduled to play Poland on March 24; the winner of that game would take on Sweden or the Czech Republic on March 29 in the battle for a ticket to the 2022 World Cup in Qatar.

It would involve a full suspension of the Russian teams, which would prevent them from participating in international tournaments. To this end, FIFA is working closely with European Football Confederation UEFA, which is also working on further sanctions. With Spartak Moscow, there is one more Russian team on the European stage this season, in the Europa League's eighth finals against RB Leipzig. In turn, the Russian women's team will be seeded for next summer's European Championships in Great Britain.

The World Football Federation already announced an initial sanctions package Sunday night, but it was not far-reaching enough for many countries. "No international competition may be finished on Russian territory anymore, home matches must be played on neutral ground and without spectators," a FIFA announcement sounded.

"In addition, the member state representing Russia will do so under the name RFU (Russian Football Union, ed.) and no longer under the name 'Russia'. At international matches of the national team, flags and national anthem are prohibited," FIFA said.

"FIFA is still holding talks with UEFA and the IOC, among others, regarding possible additional measures, such as exclusion from all competitions, if no improvement of the current situation is noticeable in the near future."

So while the World Football Federation did threaten a complete exclusion, it has not officially reached that point yet. Poland, Sweden and the Czech Republic, however, had previously indicated they did not want to play against Russia in the World Cup barrages. On Monday, they were joined by quite a few countries. England, Denmark, Ireland, Wales, Scotland, Switzerland, Albania and Norway, among others, announced they no longer wanted to play against Russia. The Royal Belgian Football Association KBVB in turn supported the refusal of Poland, Sweden and the Czech Republic to play against Russia for World Cup qualifiers at the end of March. For now, the Netherlands no longer wants to play against Russia and Belarus.

How did it happen in Qatar?

Deaths during construction work for the World Cup in Qatar are at the center of criticism of the desert emirate.

Now the world governing body FIFA has confirmed official figures: Three people are believed to have died during stadium construction. For a long time, the figure of more than 6,500 deaths has circulated since the World Cup was awarded in 2010. How can this discrepancy come about?

According to information from the organizing committee, three people have died in accidents on stadium construction sites in the host country Qatar during working hours in recent years.

This was confirmed by the soccer world federation Fifa before the start of the tournament to the Deutsche Presse-Agentur.

A further 37 deaths are said to have occurred without any direct connection to the construction work ("non-work-related deaths").

In the public debate, there was long talk of 6500 deaths since the World Cup was awarded. This figure comes from a report in the English daily newspaper "The Guardian". The truth lies in neither extreme: the figures are too low in one case and too high in the other.

Under what circumstances did the "Guardian" figure come about?

The number of deaths directly related to the World Cup is too high. In an article last February, the newspaper wrote that "more than 6500 migrant workers have died in Qatar since the World Cup was awarded."

The figure captures official data from India, Bangladesh, Nepal, Sri Lanka (a total of 5927 deaths) and Pakistan (824 deaths) from 2011 to 2020. (Work) location and cause of deaths are not specified.

The report of the English newspaper then points out that there are said to have been 37 deaths during the construction of the arenas, of which 34 are so-called non-work-related deaths with no direct connection to the work.

The "Guardian" reproduces the data of the Supreme Committee for Delivery & Legacy (short: SC), which plans and is responsible for the World Cup in the desert emirate analogous to an organizing committee.

How many deaths have there been, as of now, according to official data from the organizing committee?
In addition to the 37 deaths during the construction of the stadiums mentioned in the Guardian, three more

have occurred in 2021. Each of these cases is said to be "non-work-related deaths."

The official total thus rose to 40 in the previous year, of which 37 were "Non-Work-Related Deaths" and three were deaths directly related to stadium construction. In other words, there is no doubt that the 6500+ guest workers from the "Guardian" report died in Qatar between 2011 and 2020. However, this figure includes areas not touched by the World Cup hosting (such as domestic or hotel employees).

Nevertheless, the figure of 40 deaths officially given by the organizing committee is too small: It does not include migrant workers who died during the construction of roads and buildings or other infrastructure projects that were unquestionably implemented because of the World Cup.

This is how Nicholas McGeehan put it in the "Guardian" at the time. With his organization Fair Square, he campaigns for labor rights in the Gulf region. McGeehan said: "A very large proportion of the guest workers who have died since 2011 were only in the country because Qatar won the bid to host the World Cup."

In other words, without the World Cup, many projects would not have happened, even if they are not directly related to hosting the tournament, such as building a stadium.

40 and three: how does the World Cup organizing committee come up with its statistics?
Between 6500 ("Guardian") and 40 (official data) there is an extremely large discrepancy - and then even more, if we only assume the mentioned three deaths, which according to the SC are directly connected with the construction of the World Cup stadiums.

No more detailed information can be found on these three dead workers.

But: A look into the publications of the organizing committee clarifies how the organizer interprets whether the death is directly related to the work or not. For example, it says: "On June 29, a 38-year-old Indian man who worked as a carpenter at Lusail Stadium was transported to the hospital during the break with dizziness (...) and chest pain (...), where he later suffered cardiac arrest and died." This is one of three deaths in 2021 that SC counts as "Non-Work-Related Deaths."

A second man, a 21-year-old Indian man, died in the hospital in mid-August after being found unresponsive in his room. Official cause of death: multiple organ failure and cardiac arrest. In early October, a 47-year-old Pakistani man got out of an excavator because he "felt unwell," according to the SC document.

He collapsed next to his work equipment and could not be resuscitated. Official cause of death: acute heart failure due to natural causes. A proximity to construction site activity can hardly be denied, but the SC declares them as "Non-Work-Related Deaths."

In half of the 34 other deaths that are said to be not directly related to work, the cause of death was not even investigated in the first place; in the other half, cardiac arrest is frequently documented - although it is not likely to be the cause, but simply the determination of the end of life.

What do those responsible for the World Cup organizing committee say?
Mahmoud Qutub is the man responsible for safeguarding the rights of those who work or have worked on World Cup construction sites. He serves as the SC's executive director for labor rights. Qutub studied in Washington, D.C., and later earned a Master of Business Administration degree in Durham, North Carolina.

Speaking in perfect English to media representatives, in which RND participated, he explains that the causes of death of deceased workers are reviewed according to established procedures ("Incident Investigation Procedure").

He says, "In some cases, family members did not want an autopsy to be performed." According to the report, the causes of death were not determined in about half of the "non-work-related deaths."

Qutub also stressed that there was a comprehensible distinction of deaths according to whether they were directly or indirectly related to construction work.

Qatar emir Tamim Al Thani speaks of "unprecedented campaign"
Some four weeks before the start of the World Cup, Qatar's ruler has once again complained about the level of criticism levelled at his country in the run-up to the tournament. "Since we have had the honor of hosting the World Cup, Qatar has been subjected to an unprecedented campaign that no host country has ever experienced," Emir Tamim Bin Hamad Al Thani said Tuesday in the capital Doha.

Just under a month before the start of the World Cup in Qatar, FIFA reports a total of three deaths on stadium construction sites. The 37 other deaths are not said to be directly related to the work. This statistic differs widely from the death toll reported in British media.

According to information from the organizing committee, three people have died in accidents on stadium construction sites in World Cup host country Qatar during working hours in recent years. FIFA confirmed this a good month before the start of the tournament (Nov. 20-Dec. 18) in response to an inquiry from Deutsche Presse-Agentur. It said 37 other deaths had been recorded, these workers had not died while working on construction sites. The organizing committee therefore classifies these cases as "non-work-related deaths" - deaths that were not directly related to work.

British media reports had written of thousands of dead workers in hangovers over the years since the World Cup was awarded in December 2010. The emirate criticizes this account for failing to differentiate between the deaths and points to numerous reforms. These in turn have been criticized by human rights organizations. Amnesty International and Human Rights Watch are also calling for the establishment of a compensation fund, which the German Football Association also supports.

DFB President Bernd Neuendorf will travel to Qatar with German Interior Minister Nancy Faeser (SPD) at the end of October. "The trip will focus on the human rights issues that will be discussed around the tournament, such as the protection of queer people from discrimination and persecution, as well as the responsibility for migrant workers who built the World Cup stadiums," a spokeswoman for the federal interior minister had said.

Ahead of the World Cup in Qatar, there continues to be sharp criticism of the host. In particular, human rights violations in the country are a frequent point of criticism. Amnesty International, an organization that advocates human rights, protested in front of the

Brandenburg Gate on Sunday and demanded compensation from FIFA.

With an art action at the Brandenburg Gate, Amnesty International drew attention to human rights violations in Qatar just under a month before the start of the World Cup. At the same time, the organization called on FIFA, the world governing body, to take responsibility and to work for compensation. Participants in the protest stretched out a clothesline and hung T-shirts on it with terms such as press censorship, forced labor, discrimination, trade union bans and judicial arbitrariness. Qatar is hosting the World Cup from Nov. 20 to Dec. 18.

The wealthy emirate has been repeatedly criticized for systematic human rights abuses and the exploitation of migrants. According to Amnesty, some two million migrant workers live and work in Qatar, and hundreds of thousands of them are involved in World Cup projects. The government rejects the accusations and cites reforms in favor of the workers.

Amnesty wants FIFA to advocate for a compensation mechanism. Under the slogan "Football yes. Exploitation no", payments of at least 440 million US dollars are to be made available.

Slaves or workers?

Discrimination, starvation wages, mistreatment: A new report on working conditions at World Cup construction sites in Qatar paints a frightening picture.

London. A human rights organization has presented new detailed allegations of exploitation of workers at World Cup stadiums in Qatar. Workers from low-wage countries have been subjected to discrimination, not paid their wages and abused and mistreated, according to the report published Thursday by London-based organization Equidem.

For the 75-page report, the organization said it spoke to 60 workers over a two-year period, all of whom wished to remain anonymous.

Their accounts suggested that labor market reforms adopted by Qatar in the years leading up to the World Cup were being ignored in many cases in reality.

They reported having to pay placement fees for employment, leaving them heavily in debt before they even started. Long workdays in sweltering heat were the order of the day, they said, and Africans and people from southern Asia had to do the most dangerous work.

Protests or the formation of unions were forbidden. They were afraid to complain, because otherwise they could have lost their jobs, the workers reported.

Qatar speaks of inaccuracies and misinterpretations
The report's lead author, Namrata Raju, said spectators
should be aware that the stadiums they sit in were
created under conditions that could be described, at
least in part, as forced labor or a form of modern-day
slavery. Amnesty International and Human Rights
Watch have documented similar abuses.

Asked about Equidem's report, Qatar's media office said
that 3700 inspections had been carried out and labor
protections enforced in October alone. The body
responsible for hosting the World Cup, the Supreme
Committee for the Implementation and Legacy of the
Tournament, said the Equidem report was full of
inaccuracies and misinterpretations. Reforms since
2014 have significantly improved the situation of
workers, he said.

A French construction company was officially
investigated this week for possible human rights abuses
at World Cup construction sites in Qatar. The
allegations involve forced labor, inhumane living and
working conditions, and inadequate pay for migrant
workers.

Investigations against French company: Modern slave
labor on World Cup construction sites?
In a few days, the World Cup will begin in Qatar - and
once again, reports of devastating working conditions
on World Cup construction sites are making headlines.

Official investigations have now been launched against a French construction company.

Hanover/Paris. A French construction company has been officially investigated for possible human rights violations on World Cup construction sites in Qatar. The accusations involve forced labor, inhumane living and working conditions and insufficient payment of migrant workers, the human rights organization Sherpa announced on Wednesday.

A spokeswoman for the public prosecutor's office in Nanterre, near Paris, confirmed to CNN on Thursday the investigations ordered by a judge against Vinci Construction Grands Projets, a subsidiary of French construction group Vinci.

Employees of Sherpa said they traveled to Qatar as early as 2014 to gather evidence of allegedly inadequate working conditions at World Cup construction sites. In its statement, the human rights organization cites forced labor during extreme heat above 45 degrees and without a supply of water, passport deprivation and poor housing conditions with inadequate sanitation and no air conditioning, among other things.

The complaint, filed in 2019 and naming twelve former construction workers as witnesses, was joined by the French human rights organization Comité contre l'Esclavage Moderne.

"Companies are not above the law. This indictment sends a strong signal against the impunity of multinational corporations. It shows that the use of forced labor in their value chains can be prosecuted," Sherpa executive director Sandra Cossart is quoted as saying in the statement.

Criticism of working conditions on World Cup construction sites for years
A lawyer for Vinci Construction Grands Projets denied the allegations to CNN and announced they would challenge the judge's decision to allow investigations. He faulted lack of time to prepare for this week's hearing and spoke of insufficient evidence to support the allegations.

Since the World Cup was awarded to Qatar (Nov. 20-Dec. 18), criticism has regularly been raised over the human rights situation there and the situation of the many workers from around the world. The British "Guardian" reported at the beginning of 2021 about 6500 dead workers from five Asian countries on the emirate's construction sites in the past ten years.

On Thursday, a human rights organization also presented new, detailed allegations of exploitation of workers in the World Cup stadiums. Workers from low-wage countries have been subjected to discrimination, not paid their wages and abused and mistreated, said the report by Equidem, a London-based organization.

47

For the 75-page report, the organization said it spoke to 60 workers over a two-year period, all of whom wished to remain anonymous.

FIFA must take responsibility?

To compensate for the exploitation and death of migrant workers on World Cup construction sites, human rights organizations are demanding that Qatar and Fifa set up a compensation fund. The desert emirate has so far refused to make such a payment. Human Rights Watch is making a clear demand of the World Football Association.

Wenzel Michalski, Germany director of Human Rights Watch, has put the onus on the world soccer federation to set up a compensation fund for victims at construction sites for the World Cup in Qatar. "Fifa has to step into the breach. There they can not simply say: if the government does not participate, we evade responsibility," says Michalski to the RedaktionsNetzwerk Deutschland (RND).

Together with Amnesty International, the human rights organization is demanding a payment of 440 million euros. The desert emirate and Fifa should pay for the guest workers who were exploited on World Cup construction sites or lost their lives. The sum is equivalent to the prize money for the 32 national teams participating in the World Cup. "It's not just about the deaths during stadium construction, but overall during the construction of the infrastructure for the World Cup," Michalski emphasizes.

Qatar's Labor Minister Ali bin Samich Al Marri had recently called the call for a compensation fund a "publicity stunt." "Every death is a tragedy," Al Marri acknowledged, but stressed, "There are no criteria to establish these funds. Where are the victims? Do you have the names of the victims? How do you get these numbers?" From Human Rights Watch, therefore, there is once again a clear demand in the direction of Fifa shortly before the start of the World Cup. "This is not just a moral obligation, but a legal obligation. The employer must pay for families of workers who have died or are now unable to work."

Officially, three deaths at World Cup construction sites According to official data from the organizing committee, three deaths are reported to have occurred at stadium construction sites. In addition, there is talk of 37 other deaths that are named as "non-work-related," meaning that, according to the organizer, they were not in direct cooperation with the construction work. According to a report in the English daily newspaper "Guardian" from the beginning of last year, more than 6,500 migrant workers from India, Pakistan, Nepal and Bangladesh have died since the tournament was awarded in 2010.

The World Cup in Qatar's capital Doha kicks off Nov. 20, with the final taking place Dec. 18. The desert emirate has come under heavy criticism not only for its treatment of migrant workers, but also with regard to the rights of women and the LGBTQ+ community.

According to DFB President Bernd Neuendorf, the world governing body FIFA must also face up to its responsibility for workers who suffered accidents during the construction of the World Cup stadiums in Qatar. This is also a responsibility that the DFB must face up to, Neuendorf stressed at an award ceremony held by the DFB on Monday.

According to DFB President Bernd Neuendorf, world soccer's governing body FIFA must face up to its responsibility for those workers who died or were injured during the construction of the World Cup stadiums in Qatar and are now unable to feed their families. This is also a responsibility that the DFB must face up to, Neuendorf said on Monday evening at the Julius Hirsch Awards ceremony of the German Football Association (DFB) in Dresden.

He had also discussed the matter with FIFA President Gianni Infantino during his trip to Qatar. He said the awarding of the tournament was viewed very critically. "I think the tournament has already changed the sport," Neuendorf said. In the future, he said, the awarding will also have to be based on human rights criteria. That will be an important criterion for FIFA, he said. "That means the sport has become more political," Neuendorf explained, speaking of a good development. Soccer must raise its voice, he said. The World Cup in the emirate begins Nov. 20 and ends Dec. 18.

This year, the DFB honored, among others, the district league club SV Blau-Weiß Grana from Zeitz in Saxony-Anhalt with the Julius Hirsch Award. The club had taken in many refugees. Other award winners include the Lernort Stadion education network from Berlin and the Erinnerungsarbeit network in the context of Hamburger SV. The honorary prize went to Burak Yilmaz, an educator and author from Duisburg.

The DFB has been commemorating Jewish victims of the Nazi regime with this award every year since 2005. Individuals, clubs and institutions are honored for their commitment to combating anti-Semitism and discrimination. The award is named after Julius Hirsch. He was a DFB national player, Olympic participant and two-time German champion. He was murdered in Auschwitz in 1943.

In the so-called kafala system, employers ("sponsors") exercise an excessive degree of control over migrant workers and their legal status. Until recently, migrant workers were only allowed to change jobs or leave the country with the consent of their employers. Due to the extreme dependency on their employers, workers can hardly defend themselves against exploitation, abuse and mistreatment. They are completely at the mercy of their sponsors.

Although the kafala regulation has now been abolished by law in Qatar, it continues to be applied in practice and the abolition is increasingly being called into question again. Qatar has abolished the requirement for an exit permit and a No Objection Certificate (NOC) for most migrant workers, theoretically allowing them to leave the country and change jobs without seeking the consent of their sponsors. But de facto, employers still have the ability to block workers from changing jobs and control their legal status. Withholding wages and benefits also makes it difficult for workers to leave the workplace. Migrant workers continue to depend on their employers to enter and stay in Qatar. Employers can still file lawsuits for "leaving the workplace without permission" and cancel residence permits - practices that are abused to control the workforce.

For migrant workers who are exploited, it is difficult to claim their rights or receive compensation. They are not allowed to join unions and thus cannot fight together for better working conditions.

Should we boycott sporting events in countries with questionable human rights records? Ever since the World Cup was awarded to Qatar 10 years ago, there have been calls for a boycott due to the precarious human rights situation. Soccer fans, players and clubs are calling for the withdrawal of support for the World Cup in Qatar, expressing their protest against FIFA's decision and the exploitation of migrants. The human rights concerns are too great, the aftertaste of a joyous soccer festival in the midst of injustice too bitter - the reasons for boycotting a sporting event like the World Cup in Qatar are obvious.

At the same time, major sporting events like the World Cup also have the potential to make human rights abuses visible and bring about improvements. The FIFA World Cup is one of the most watched sporting events in the world. In 2018, more than half of the world's population watched the World Cup. Amnesty International has made a conscious decision not to boycott the World Cup in Qatar, choosing instead to use the world's attention as an opportunity for positive change. We want to focus this attention on those who make this major event possible in the first place - migrant workers. Our role as a human rights organization is to document the dramatic situation of migrant workers around the World Cup, to raise global awareness of their suffering, and to build pressure on those responsible to bring about change. We are using the time leading up to the World Cup to highlight the exploitation of migrant workers, demand reforms and improve their situation.

As a result of the reporting, Qatar has already taken important steps to better protect workers - important steps, but obviously only a first start. With international pressure mounting in recent years, the Qatari government committed in 2017 to abolish the kafala system and initiate other important reforms. Since then, important progress has indeed been made in Qatar, with the introduction of new legal frameworks and initiatives that improve the situation of migrant workers. These include a law regulating working hours for domestic workers, labor courts to facilitate access to justice, a fund to pay for unpaid wages, and a minimum wage. Qatar has also abolished laws that previously required migrant workers to obtain permission from their employers to change jobs or leave the country. Two important human rights treaties have been ratified (though without recognizing the right to form trade unions). If fully implemented, these reforms can help eliminate the most problematic aspects of the kafala system and enable migrant workers to escape exploitative and abusive working conditions and claim compensation.

But since then, there has also been regression and stagnation. Despite the reform processes that have been initiated, the daily lives of many migrant workers in Qatar remain harsh and exploitation continues - partly because announced reforms have not yet been effectively implemented. It is therefore high time for Qatar to finally deliver on these promises - and FIFA must also live up to its responsibility. As the World Cup organizer, FIFA must publicly speak out and demand that the Qatari government implement its labor reform program before the opening match of the World Cup. Amnesty International will not tire of publicly reminding FIFA of its responsibilities.

Qatar wants to buy recognition?

Jochen Breyer's film "Secret Affair Qatar" raised a lot of dust even before it was broadcast on Tuesday evening. "You think being gay is a sin?" asked Breyer of one of Qatar's World Cup ambassadors, former soccer star Khalid Salman. The only Qatari he was allowed to visit on the ground - where media relations are strictly controlled. "Yes, mental damage," the man replied. The Qatari supervisor for Breyer's ZDF film team actually wanted to stop the interview beforehand. Namely, at the moment when the conversation turned to gay World Cup guests, who are "not allowed" according to Qatari law.

"Khalid is not the best person to comment on the law," the attendant of the official World Cup organizing committee interrupts the interview. No more questions about that! But Khalid Salman has not yet said everything that is important to him. He goes on talking about how it would be a problem if children saw gays. "Because it is a damage in the mind", in German roughly: "Being gay is a mental damage."

In general, Jochen Breyer brings amazing insights from the desert state in his documentary "Geheimsache Qatar": Also about the connection of the German Bundesliga to Qatar and the European top club association "European Club Association" in particular. According to the ZDF documentary's research, Karl-Heinz Rummenigge, who headed the association until

2017, came into play when the World Cup award to Qatar, which was decided in 2010, came under massive pressure in the following years. Many European soccer big players such as the English Premier League spoke out against a winter World Cup in Qatar. It would never have been possible to play at 40 to 50 degrees in the summer anyway.

The rules in Qatar

In many European countries, soccer is the number one national sport and therefore an emotional topic for many people. At the World Cup in particular, the entire nation is usually rooting for its own team, cheering for the team and celebrating the players like heroes. At the controversial World Cup in Qatar, however, there is much more to talk about besides the sport.

The emirate is facing accusations of various human rights violations and is being criticized for this from many sides.

Guest workers have lost their lives on World Cup construction sites, and the numbers range from a few to thousands. However, no one in Qatar really wants to take responsibility for the deaths.

To see for herself on the ground, German Interior Minister Nancy Faeser was in Qatar. After her visit, she drew a positive conclusion.

The Qatari Prime Minister had given her a security guarantee for every visitor to the World Cup, including homosexuals. Nevertheless, it is important for soccer fans to follow some rules in the emirate.

We show you the most important rules you need to know about alcohol consumption, dress code, sexuality and general behavior in public.

Can you drink alcohol in Qatar?
Fifa has negotiated with the Qatari organizers where and by whom alcohol may be consumed as an exception during the World Cup. Normally, alcohol is absolutely taboo throughout the country, but Qatar has based its ban on the Koran.

Alcoholic beverages will not be served in the stadiums themselves. Instead, alcohol will be available for purchase and consumption in certain outdoor areas of the stadium before and after the games. In addition, there will be a fan mile where alcoholic beverages will be sold from 6:30 p.m., he said.

Certain bars or restaurants will also have the option of selling alcohol to people who can prove they are older than 21. To accommodate fans, cruise ships are anchored in the port of Doha, and alcoholic beverages may also be served on board them.

Despite these exceptions, however, it is important for all visitors to respect the local culture, the organizers said. Those who are too drunk must expect to be taken to certain areas to sober up. Public urination is punishable by fines, they said, and drug use or trafficking face much harsher penalties.

What is the dress code in Qatar?
During the World Cup, Qatar will have summer temperatures around 25 degrees Celsius and higher.

However, summer clothing will not be the order of the day for fans on site, the host made that clear relatively early on. Clothing should cover the body at least from the shoulders to the knees, and deep necklines are also not desired.

Swimming trunks, bikinis or even topless clothing is only allowed at pools or beaches where this is explicitly mentioned.

Is kissing allowed in public in Qatar?
In short, anything beyond holding hands is not welcome in public. The travel portal "qatar-travel" points this out. This includes kissing, but also hugging. Who acts against it, must count on punishments.

The fact that prostitution is also forbidden and severely punished is no longer surprising.

What rules apply to homosexuals in Qatar?
Homosexuality is illegal in Qatar. According to the German Foreign Office, LGBTQI+ travelers should be aware that in the Islamic state "homosexual acts and non-marital sexual intercourse are prohibited and punishable by criminal law."

So even if the Federal Minister of the Interior was given a guarantee of safety for all World Cup soccer fans, each person must be aware that showing same-sex affection in public can result in much more drastic penalties than for heterosexual people. Homosexual acts can be punished by up to seven years in prison, and theoretically the death penalty is also possible under Sharia law, but there are no known cases in which this has been applied.

After homophobic statements by Qatar's World Cup ambassador Salman, the Lesbian and Gay Association (LSVD), among others, expressed concern for the safety of LGBTQI+ people. A requested travel warning for the group of people in question has now nevertheless been rejected by the German Foreign Office.

Same-sex couples who want to book a hotel room together must therefore expect to be rejected. The best chances of getting a room in Qatar for homosexual couples are with international hotel chains. The booking platform "misterb&b" lists LGBTQI+-friendly accommodations worldwide, and travelers can also find hotels for Qatar through it.

Are political statements or criticism allowed in Qatar? That criticism of Qatar is not welcome in the emirate has become relatively clear in recent weeks. Again and again, World Cup organizers as well as politicians of the country complained about how other countries would judge them. For this reason, local soccer fans should hold back on political statements or criticism.